Mr R S Hawkins
46 Birch Grove
DUNFERMLINE
KY11 5BE

TG6/AG3

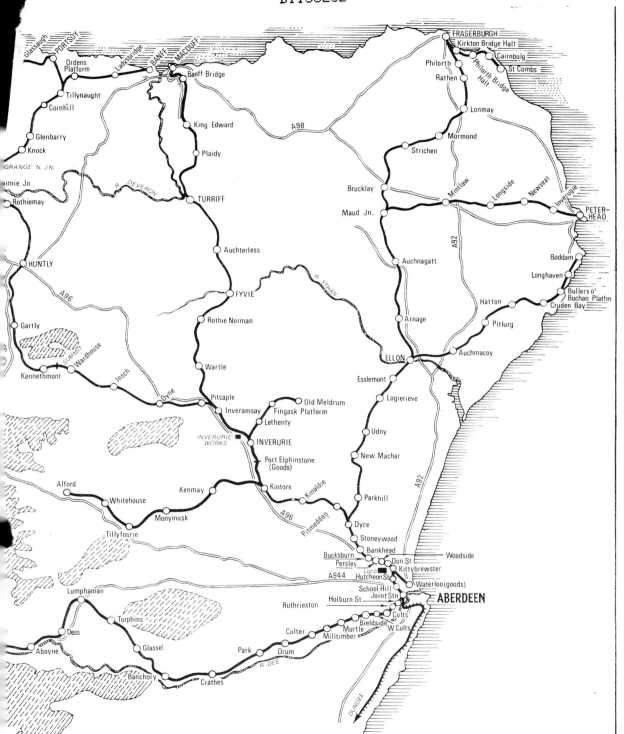

GREAT NORTH OF SCOTLAND RAILWAY ALBUM

A.E. Glen, I.A. Glen
with
A.G. Dunbar

GREAT NORTH OF SCOTLAND RAILWAY COMPANY

FRASER STEWART BOOKS

Preface

First published 1960 by Ian Allan Ltd

ISBN 1-85648-188-3

This edition published 1994 by
Fraser Stewart Book Wholesale Ltd,
Waltham Abbey, Essex.
Produced by the Promotional Reprint Company Limited.

Printed in India

The authors wish to thank all those who have
given valuable help with the compilation of this
album. In the first place, some unpublished
extracts concerning railway events in the
Scottish North-East have been drawn from
Royal Archives, as the Great North of Scotland
Railway was so closely associated with Royal
holidays. These extracts together with the top
photograph on p46 are reproduced with the
gracious permission of Her Majesty the Queen.
Miss Langton at the Royal Archives is thanked
for her enthusiastic assistance.

Several photographs in this *Great North of
Scotland Railway Album* have been taken by
Mr A. Ernest Glen and are his copyright. Others
have been drawn from the Glen Collection. Mr
Alan G. Dunbar, who is a well known authority
on the Great North, has offered his Dunbar
Collection for selection. Once again our warm
thanks go to him for his participation in the
preparation of this book.

Mr W. E. Boyd, Mr A. G. Ellis, Mr G. E.
Langmuir and Mr J. L. Stevenson have also
most generously assisted us with information
and illustrations. Mr John Peter has prepared
the bulk of the photographs for this book and
the pleasing results stem from his patient
efforts.

To other railway enthusiasts and
organisations which have allowed their
photographs to be reproduced, grateful
acknowledgement is made:

D. M. Burton, G. H. Croughton, J. A. N. Emslie,
G. H. Robin, J. G. Sellar, Hamish Stevenson,
Ian Allan Limited, British Rail, David & Charles
Limited, The Locomotive Club of Great Britain
(Ken Nunn Collection), The Mitchell Library.

Introduction

The Great North of Scotland Railway, in spite of its rather pretentious title, was Scotland's smallest regional rail system, its lines only amounted to $334\frac{1}{4}$ miles. The venture was launched in 1844 in the full flush of enthusiasm that is now remembered as the 'Railway Mania', when so many railway company promotions began. Then the boom collapsed and the Great North's Aberdonian promoters, who were rightly 'canny' with their 'sillar', had second thoughts about the project. Hence the Great North was a long time a-building, and 10 years elapsed before the first train ran.

The Great North was inspired by a rather grand scheme — the intention being to make a line from Aberdeen to Inverness and in 1846 the Great North obtained an Act of Parliament for that purpose. At that time a proposal for a route from Perth to Inverness by a rival company was rejected on account of the long, steep inclines through the Grampians — much to the chagrin of the citizens of Inverness and the Northern Counties. A quantum of ill feeling was generated as the Highlanders saw no reason why they should have to travel to Perth through Aberdeen, thereby putting 67 miles on

to their journey. The animosity was to continue for many years. When the Inverness & Nairn Railway, for example, attempted to collaborate with the Great North in 1855 to form a through line between the cities, the parties still could not agree.

The Great North of Scotland Railway was by no means the first line to appear in the north-east. That honour belonged to the Aberdeen Railway which was opened from the Granite City to Forfar on 1 April 1850. Then the Morayshire Railway, linking Elgin and Lossiemouth, was opened for traffic on 10 August 1852 and it was quickly followed by another new line which was in business as far as Banchory by 8 September 1853.

Eventually the Great North of Scotland subscribers put up a sufficiency of money, contractors were appointed and the first sod was cut at Westhall, near Oyne in the valley of the Don, on 25 November 1852. The portion of the line from Huntly to Inverurie was built first, because part of the Aberdeen-Port Elphinstone Canal was to form the track bed and the canal was to be kept intact as long as possible. Construction of the railway was not uneventful, for the contractor, being anxious to press on with the work, cut into the bank of the canal, letting the water run out into the River Don stopping all the barges. The canal had to be refilled to refloat them!

The Great North's first section was formally opened to Huntly on 19 September 1854. A special train consisting of 25 little coaches drawn by two engines left Kittybrewster, near Aberdeen, at eleven o'clock. It conveyed the Board members and officers of the railway together with other gentlemen at fares 'fixed at one and a half the ordinary fare' to make the event rather exclusive. The excursion took no less than two hours to reach Huntly.

From 1856 onwards many extensions were made to the rail network for the North-East of

Left: The crest of the Great North of Scotland Railway was an impressive one, including the Scottish royal lions in two quarters and the three castles of the Aberdeen armorial bearings in the other two. It was only after 1920, however, that a transfer of the crest began to appear on locomotive splashers, notably on the Class F of 1920-1 *J. Peter Collection*

Scotland. First a link was formed with Keith (1856); the Banff, Macduff and Turriff line was built (1860); the Formartine and Buchan was constructed to Peterhead and Fraserburgh (1862); and the route from Rothes to Elgin was completed (1862). Soon the railway was formed as far as Nethybridge (1863). But the most controversial extension was that involving the Aboyne & Braemar Railway, a continuation of the track from Banchory.

Queen Victoria had first travelled over the new line from Banchory in October 1853 shortly after its commissioning. After two changes of horses, at Ballater and Aboyne, the station was reached. The Queen commented: 'At Banchory we got into the train, going by a line which is quite new and has only been open a few weeks. It passes close to Aberdeen and is a great improvement.' By the summer of 1860 it was possible for the royal party to travel to Aboyne from the south. On that occasion so fearsome were the noises of the engines that the horses ran away from the station, taking the royal carriage with them, but all was well. Thus the tracks were coming ever closer to Balmoral Castle.

In 1864, Colonel James Farquharson, the owner of Invercauld estate, which was near Balmoral but on the opposite bank of the river, proposed to give his support to a scheme to extend the railway from Aboyne through Ballater to Braemar. He had inherited a debt of about £100,000 (some of which he had cleared), and stood to gain about £2,500 a year if the railway was built near his land and used to transport timber from his forests. The scheme hinged upon his joining the venture as Chairman, taking payment for all his land in shares, and taking further shares to be bought out of the profits he would make by the increased returns from his woods. The building of the railway would, therefore, be very much to his advantage; he was anxious, however, to consult Queen Victoria's views on the subject, and would do nothing which was against her wishes.

This put the Queen in an embarrassing situation. She was most anxious that Colonel Farquharson should not act against what he thought to be his best interests, but at the same time she was completely opposed to the whole project. In a letter to Colonel Farquharson of 14 December 1864, Sir Charles Phipps, Keeper of the Privy Purse wrote:
'The Queen feels so strongly upon the subject of the Railway that she thinks its existence in the neighbourhood of Balmoral would go far to destroy all her enjoyment of the Palace.'
It was of course quite impossible that Colonel Farquharson should be seen to give up an advantageous project solely on account of the Queen's wishes, particularly as she naturally wished to remain on good terms with all her neighbours. There were, however, a number of objections. First, the existence of a railway a very short way from Balmoral, and along the whole north side of the valley, would seriously damage Balmoral as a pleasant, peaceful residence. The country would have floods of tourists and the passage of trains close to the road would cause the driving of horses to be unsafe. No pecuniary advantage could be gained, as there was no timber at Balmoral of a size or quantity to make its sale profitable. The Turnpike Road from Aboyne to Castleton of Braemar was now complete, and the greater part of the expense of this work had been borne by the Prince Consort. The road was beginning to pay some percentage upon the large sums laid out on it. But this revenue would cease if the road were in competition with a parallel railway, while at the same time it would nonetheless have to be maintained as if it were remunerative. Finally the Queen felt that the construction of the railway was a speculation which was bound to fail. The only obvious beneficiary was Colonel Farquharson, there was little local support, and a great many people, such as the Earl of Fife and the Marquis of Huntly, were against it.

After prolonged negotiations, during which it was proposed that the railway should merely go to Ballater, Colonel Farquharson said that he was prepared to oppose any future extension of the railway beyond Ballater if Queen Victoria would agree to make a tramway from Ballater to his forest, to be in her, and his, ownership and control, and not to be used while she was at Balmoral. With certain reservations, this was acceptable to the Queen, and an agreement was drawn up and signed in May 1865. In 1870 Queen Victoria first leased, and subsequently bought, the Ballochbuie Forest to prevent its being cut down, and in saving these fine woodlands put money into Colonel Farquharson's pocket. For passenger traffic the railway thus came no nearer to Balmoral than Ballater, and throughout its history that station, 12 miles and 4 furlongs from the castle, was always associated with royal journeyings and holidays.

Between 1866 and 1887, the Great North was the focus of several amalgamations — the Old Meldrum branch which had been leased to the GNSR was absorbed by the latter company, and then the Banffshire and Morayshire Railways joined the Great North's fold. Thus the Great North of Scotland Railway, like many another, grew out of a jumble of amalgamations and promotions, as the Buchan

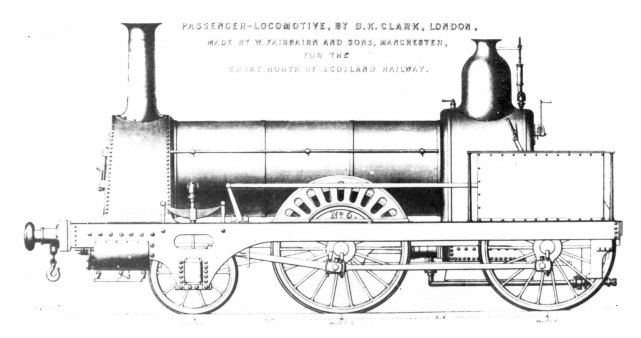

Above: For its first locomotives the Great North of Scotland Railway sought the guidance of D. K. Clark, a well-known writer on the subject who had a London office, and made only occasional visits to Aberdeen, which after all was some 500 miles away. Clark's appointment to the Great North, however, stated that he must be on hand in that city. The first offer to supply locomotives came from the firm of Blaikie Brothers of Aberdeen on 15 August 1853: 'The engine and tender we have on hand just now are very powerful and fit for any traffic,' but the local product was refused. The choice for Class 1 was a 2-4-0 with outside cylinders, and a large brass dome with Salter safety valves set on a raised firebox. Initially the little engines had open vent splashers, and lacked even a plate to protect the crew; the batch was constructed by W. Fairbairn and Sons, Manchester. Although seven locomotives were on order for the opening of the line, only four were available by September 1854, as there was a strike at the works. Design errors together with poor workmanship hindered the performance of the engines until they were rebuilt. This drawing shows No 5 as it was when new. *Clark & Colburn*

chiels learned that co-operation was better than competition.

In its early years the Great North made travel rather tough for travellers coming from the south by stubbornly refusing to have a joint station with the Aberdeen Railway, which was subsequently taken over by the Caledonian in 1866. The Great North's main line station in Aberdeen was at Waterloo but that of the Aberdeen Railway was at Guild Street; between the stations there was nearly half a mile of busy quays over which the passengers

had to hurry carrying their luggage. At times it is said they arrived panting at the GNSR station only to find the gates locked and the trains pulling out. When a passenger had the gate at Guild Street shut in his face, he rightly complained, only to be told that the trains must leave on time. To which he retorted 'Why all the fuss when they never arrive when they should?'.

In 1867 however a new joint station was established for the use of the Caley and the Great North which were eventually joined in 1883 by the North British (exercising its running powers into Aberdeen from Kinnaber Junction). The joint station was connected to the GNSR at Kittybrewster via the Denburn Valley line.

For many years the Great North of Scotland's trains took an uncomfortably long time to go places, but only some 60 miles of its entire network were double track, and the rails were of a light variety. In 1880 its best train took 4hr 15min to cover the 80 miles from Aberdeen to Elgin. The slowest train back took no less than $6\frac{1}{4}$hr for the journey, but it stopped at all the stations. The 'trainies' were wont to loiter on the way, only to make frantic efforts to catch up between the stops. One summer day a Great North train ambling towards Aberdeen was passing Hallburn where there was a cricket ground beside the line. To entertain all aboard, the train came to a halt, and some ten minutes play was enjoyed. Subsequently the driver and the guard were called to account for the delay, but by then they were not on speaking terms — so the driver reported that a buffer beam had caught fire, hence he and the fireman had to stop to put it out. But the guard wrote that the train was held up by high winds and wet rails!

The fares and freight charges were a source of annoyance to passengers and to companies who consigned goods by the Great North. A Dufftown distiller who was at war with the Company over freight rates was advised by his Elgin lawyer to start keeping sheep and ask for a composition ticket if he wanted any concessions from the GNSR! After 1880 matters improved with the appointment of Mr William G. Moffatt as General Manager, and better sense prevailed: he was described as 'large and mighty but not a bad fellow at all'. From then on, the Great North of Scotland Railway became one of the most enterprising and efficient smaller systems in the British Isles.

The Great North of Scotland Railway's traffic was subject to wide fluctuations in volume. There were seasonal peaks generated by agriculture, especially at harvest time when the corn or the 'tatties' were being gathered. The fish consignments were also variable in amount and season. The Great North had concession tickets for fish wives (with one creel), and for fishermen if they travelled on the slow trains (of which the Great North had plenty). Sometimes not only the coaches, but also the locomotives from the coastal harbours smelt of fish!

Much regular business also came from the distilleries. Almost all tracks in the system went at some point to a distillery. As a result most GNSR stations could produce a dram of the 'Real Mackay' for visitors. A favourite pursuit of the tool van squad from Elgin was the reroading of vehicles at distilleries. They became quite expert at the job. It was rumoured that such derailments could usually be arranged given a little notice. On one occasion when the squad was called out on a Friday afternoon to the Dufftown area they failed to reappear until Monday morning. Of course, they first took a sample of the whisky on the site, and then the better to appraise its worth called at every other distillery on the way home!

In the summer months there was tourism to consider. From time to time, the visitors' numbers were greatly augmented by local folk out to enjoy an excursion, on such occasions as Aberdeen's 'Trips Saturday' (the third in July) when the Great North ran a phenomenal number of trains which taxed its locomotives and rolling stock to the limits. Altogether the

Great North of Scotland Railway made an essential contribution to the economic progress and wellbeing of the communities of the Scottish North-East.

The Great North's locomotive list throughout its history only amounted to some 180 engines; these have been described as largely consisting of 'old 4-4-0s, new 4-4-0s, rebuilt 4-4-0s, 4-4-0s with superheaters, 4-4-0s with names and 4-4-0s without names'. The first locomotives of this type came to the GNSR in 1862, it being one of the first British networks to purchase the variety. They proved to be versatile, practical and economical — and such engines could be employed virtually throughout the Great North's system. Hence light 4-4-0 locomotives were to characterise that railway for almost a century. As regards the naming of the engines it was rumoured that anyone could have a name of his choice put on a Great North locomotive if he 'wud pey fur it'.

Invariably, in the old days, the tenders had a pail hanging over the side; some say the pails held tools for stopgap repairs, others say they were for cleaning purposes, but they gave a surprising domestic touch to the appearance of the engines. Equally the improvised tender cabs which were put together to give some protection when travelling in reverse (particularly on coastal workings) were quite rustic.

Most of the GNSR engines came from locomotive builders although from its beginnings the Great North had works at Kittybrewster. Only two locomotives were ever constructed there, but once the new works at Inverurie were open several engines were successfully built by the Company.

The Great North's rolling stock was for long rather spartan; its old four wheelers are said to have conveyed the impression that they rolled over the ballast! After 1880 improvements came slowly, and by 1896 the Company was pioneering the use of corridor stock. So comfortable and complete however were its new coaches that in 1903 the Great North of Scotland Railway was able to provide its own Royal Train to convey King Edward VII from Doncaster to Ballater.

There were few engineering features of note on the Great North of Scotland's system — there were valleys to span and rivers to bridge as on any upland railway — there was also some steep hills on the lines, especially in the Rothes area, and sharp inclines and curves in the valleys near Dufftown. Almost every station displayed its altitude above sea level, either over the booking office window or on the station name board, as though the Great North tracks attained Andean heights: Ellon was 58ft, Cults was 126ft, Huntly 400ft, Ballater 660ft, while Boat of Garten topped the lot at 702ft above sea level.

The Great North was enterprising — it was the scene of James Manson's experiments with the automatic tablet exchange apparatus in 1885, the first installation being at Parkhill on the Buchan route. This was to prove most advantageous to the Company not only in protecting employees from injury, but also in enabling fast trains to be run, as single-line working was so general on the Great North. The company was a pioneer in the oil firing of locomotives, in superheating, in steam railcars, and in running motorbuses to supplement train services. The Great North was the first sizeable railway to appoint a woman to an executive position, as Manageress of its Cruden Bay Hotel. Shortly before the Grouping the Great North had the honour of advertising the longest through service in Britain — from Aberdeen to Penzance, no less than 785 miles!

It was the Great North's regional, even parochial character that caught the imagination of the travelling public. The local people took a close interest in the 'trainies' and timed their days by the comings and goings on the track. This proprietorial concern was quite upset when the railway company had the effrontery in 1916 to paint its engines black; up to that time they had been green — officially a Brunswick green, and that is what its customers liked best. Then there were the personal services to regular travellers: on the coast line a frequent passenger to Garmouth was a Mr Grant. The usual driver on the train was known as Rossie. One day, as the train was pulling out, Rossie caught site of Mr Grant running towards the station, and of course he stopped the train, and shouted from the cab, 'Ca' awa, Mr Grant, I'll haud oan fur ye!' The stationmaster, who was rather officious, stalked up and told Rossie off for, 'Haudin' up the hale railway', but Rossie's withering reply was, 'Fat the sorra dae *ye* ken aboot rinnin' trainies?'

Many too were the parcels and messages that were tossed off footplates over fences as the Great North 'trainies' sauntered through the countryside of Buchan and Mar — although there were no instructions about such favours in the official Working Arrangements.

As early as 1908 the Great North was participating in joint through workings to Inverness with the Highland Railway, and amalgamation plans were in the air. But out on the tracks old rivalries were persistent — especially on the parallel lines into Boat of Garten where there was many a race between the two companies' trains. A Highland driver recounted his experiences there:
'There we were coming up from Forres with eight or nine coaches and a ''Castle'' to haal

Above: The Great North's second consignment of 2-4-0s from W. Fairbairn and Sons had an additional pillar safety valve on the boiler. In this photograph No 15 of this group is seen at Huntly c1870. The coupled wheels were 5ft 6in and the cylinders 15½in by 20in. After rebuilding by Cowan, No 15 was still active in 1884.
R. Scott

them. Jist past Broomhill yonder, the Great North train with its wee engine would come chasing along with four or five six-wheelers behind it. A young fireman I had was real angry at them when they came up on us on yon straight bit. But, och I jist said to him ''Never heed these impident fellows with their tin charlies'' — that's what we aye called the Great North engines in the Highland — we're up to time and the folk will jist have to wait on us at the Boat aal the same!'

In 1910 when it was at its peak the Great North of Scotland Railway had 115 locomotives and over 770 carriages; it carried over 3¼ million passengers a year, many of whom patronised the local trains or 'subbies' as they were familiarly known in the Aberdeen area. Its goods traffic was quite substantial, hence some 3,692 wagons were at work. Over 70% of the freight traffic is said to have come off the Caley, but the total amounted to over half a million tons of minerals (mostly coal) and almost half a million tons of general items such as livestock from the GNSR hinterland, whisky traffic from the 'triangle' of Banff and Moray, or fish traffic from the coast of Buchan.

Although the Great North of Scotland

Railway was part of the LNER group for over 20 years it retained its character throughout that regime, right on to the formation of British Railways. Back in 1922 a driver was asked about the amalgamations. His answer was 'It winna mak muckle cheenge on the North'. And he was right; instructions from London or Doncaster made little impact in Alford, Banff or Boat of Garten where staff continued to run the railway on GNSR principles. Up to the mid-1950s, Great North engines hauling Great North coaches were still to be seen puffing along the rural and coastal by-ways of the North-East.

In *The Reshaping of British Railways*, (The Beeching Report of 1963), it was proposed that the old Great North network be severely truncated. As a result of the implementation of that report, only a fragment of the system remains today. The GNSR main line is still followed to Keith, but thereafter the former Highland route to Elgin is used. From Cairnie Junction the branch to Dufftown is intact but it is only open for goods traffic as are two other short lengths of track.

Yet much nostalgia for the Great North is to be found; of its neat and practical locomotives No 49 *Gordon Highlander* has been preserved and may be seen in Glasgow's Museum of Transport. Furthermore, the Great North is one of only two pre-Grouping Scottish railways to boast an association of its own. This volume attempts to portray the character of the Great North of Scotland Railway in its various guises through the century of its history.

Above: A view at Waterloo station, Aberdeen, of one of the 0-4-0 well-tank locomotives which were built for the Great North by Beyer, Peacock and Company in 1855-6. Originally these little engines were cabless and were mainly engaged in banking passenger and goods trains from the old Waterloo station out to Kittybrewster. The coach is a box-like four-compartment four-wheeler typical of Great North coaching stock at this time. Waterloo station was closed to passenger traffic in 1867. *L&GRP*

Below: At first the little 0-4-0 well-tanks were mainly employed in banking at Aberdeen. Both locomotives were rebuilt, first by Cowan in 1876, without any alteration in appearances; and then by Pickersgill who gave them new boilers, and located the dome and safety valves on the centre of the barrel instead of on the raised firebox. He also chose an enclosed cab in place of a spectacle plate. Latterly this engine carrying No 13A, was working at Elgin where this photograph was taken c1910, while the other, No 14A, was similarly engaged at Keith. *A. G. Dunbar Collection*

Above left: After hire to the War Department in 1915 for construction of a line to an airship station at Lenabo (the branch left the Maud route at Longside) No 14A and its sister were sold to a Glasgow firm. Further war service followed at a shell-filling factory at Chilwell, after which this locomotive went to a colliery in South Wales. It was known as *Julian;* it was in action up to 1943! *LPC*

Below left: No 24 was one of the Class 19 (or B) 2-4-0 type locomotives to appear on the Great North. These were the first engines W. Cowan, the Locomotive Superintendent from 1858 to 1883, bought for the railway. They were built by Robert Stephenson and Company, Newcastle between 1859 and 1861. At the outset there was only a spectacle plate to give the train crew some shelter. A curious fitment on these engines were the injector clack boxes on the front ring of the boiler — ostensibly to keep cold water away from the firebox! No 24 was subsequently rebuilt in 1882 with larger cylinders, a bigger boiler and a proper cab — part of the policy of economy which prevailed for many a year. *A. G. Ellis Collection*

Above: The Old Meldrum branch was famous because of the redoubtable locomotives which frequented it. They all won the title 'Meldrum Meg' from a reference by a local poet to the engine on the branch line there. Here No 19, the 2-4-0 which gave its designation to its class, is seen at the platform at Old Meldrum c1890. The curious metal spout to assist filling the tender, which held only 950gal of water, plus two tons of coal, is clearly seen in this picture. *A. G. Dunbar Collection*

Below: The final three locomotives on order from Stephenson to complete Class 19 were altered to the 4-4-0 wheel arrangement, which was quite an innovation in 1859. Bogies were put on Nos 28-30 at a cost of £130, but delivery was not effected until January 1862. Another six engines of the same type to be known as Class 28 or H were also placed on contract. The cylinders were 16in by 22in while the coupled wheels were 5ft 1in. These locomotives were found to be well suited to sinuous lines such as those in Buchan or in the Craigellachie area. The photograph shows No 29 in rebuilt form after a cab had been built (in lieu of a small spectacle plate) and a Westinghouse pump installed. *Glen Collection*

Right: Once in Great North control, the motive power of the railways with which it amalgamated was soon replaced as this was the policy of the Great North board. In this picture an 0-4-2 locomotive which came from Hawthorn and Company, Leith, in 1857, appears as GNS No 51 and it continued in service until 1878. It is thought that the gentleman on the footplate is Mr W. Cowan, the Great North's Locomotive Superintendent.
A. G. Dunbar Collection

Right: The Morayshire Railway became part of the Great North in 1863; only two engines were thought fit for inclusion in the GNS list, although four were extant. A split among the Morayshire shareholders in 1858 had led to the purchase of two locomotives from Neilson and Company by Mr James Grant of Glengrant, who began a separate line from Elgin to Rothes. The engines were 2-4-0 side and saddle tanks with 5ft 1in coupled wheels. The first of these was *Glen Grant* which was built in 1859. When it joined the Great North it became No 41 and was sent to the Old Meldrum branch, where it sojourned until 1885.
Glen Collection

Right: Having proved the virtues of the 4-4-0 wheel arrangement the Great North became one of its staunchest supporters. When new locomotives for the Fraserburgh route were bought from Neilson and Company, Glasgow, in 1866 they followed the new pattern. The brass dome and the copper cap on the chimney, together with brass work on the boiler and splashers had now become the customary Great North style as this Neilson official picture shows. On Class 43, or K as it became known, the cab however was rudimentary. *Mitchell Library*

Above: When Class 43, or K, came to be rebuilt the engines received flush top boilers on which the dome was relocated in the centre of the barrel. A dummy valve seat on the firebox gave steam for the injectors. Six-wheel tenders were also constructed. This photograph shows No 44 of this class, after its modernisation in 1890. *LPC*

Below: The rebuilt Class K locomotives found employment in various capacities. About 1921, No 48 joined the Civil Engineer's section and a second Westinghouse pump with an air cylinder was installed to give compressed air for pneumatic tools such as riveting or spike-driving machines. No 48 was put on the duplicate list (becoming No 48A) and this view shows the engine at Inverurie complete with its gadgetry. *A. G. Dunbar Collection*

Above: Many veteran Great North locomotives had their appearance transformed by reconstruction — a policy followed mainly in the interests of economy. No 45 however was rebuilt in 1891 but much on its original lines. This photograph dates from the early 1920s and shows the locomotive with its small four-wheel tender with outside springs and framing, plus rear toolbox and safety chains (as a precaution against breakage of couplings). *Glen Collection*

Below: By 1873 there was a shortage of locomotives on the Great North. W. Cowan, the locomotive chief, placed an order for six new engines with Neilson and Company unbeknown to the GNSR board. One may judge of the members' surprise when the facts were discovered two years after the event! The Class 49 or L locomotives appeared in 1876; they were basically just a larger version of Class 43 (K), but they had six-wheel tenders from the outset, and at long last the Great North had proper cabs installed on the engines. The coupled wheels were 5ft 6½in, while the cylinders were 17in by 24in. No 57 is seen in this photograph in its original form. *Mitchell Library*

Above: A close-up of No 55 of Class L shows the locomotive after the fitting of the Westinghouse brake. The elaborate livery which was the Great North fashion in the 1890s is seen to advantage in this photograph. *LPC*

Below: With the grey granite tenements of Kittybrewster as a background, No 54 of Cowan's Class L awaits employment c 1896. The brass dome and copper cap on the chimney, together with the mountings on the splashers and the boiler gave the cleaning staffs plenty of work. The rod attachment to the handrail is thought to be a mechanism to activate a blower ring in the chimney. After reconstruction in 1897 No 54 (as No 54A) saw service until 1924. *A. G. Dunbar Collection*

15

Above: When the Class 49 or L class engines came to be reconstructed from 1897 onwards during William Pickersgill's term of office, a flush top boiler was again chosen, with modern mountings, including Ramsbottom safety valves. This photograph of No 55 (p15) taken c1910, therefore makes a remarkable 'before and after' comparison with the picture of the same locomotive taken 30 years before. The setting is again Kittybrewster with the sheer legs and part of the roundhouse in the background.   *LPC*

Below: No 52 of the rather elegant L class 4-4-0s was delivered in 1876. A drastic reconstruction took place in 1897 when Pickersgill was in charge; new boiler mountings were used, and No 52 eventually received a unique second-hand cab with side windows from No 54. It is seen here c1900 in the Brunswick green livery of that time.   *LPC*

Above: As traffic continued to boom in the 1870s the inadequacy of the locomotive stock on the Great North became apparent. In November 1877 an order was placed with Neilson and Company for a further 12 locomotives. Nine of these became Class 57 (or M). While the boiler was the same as Class L, the cylinders were enlarged to 17½in by 26in, which was to prove a weakness until the locomotives were rebuilt. As the Great North track was light, the rails being of 72lb/yd section, the axle load was only 14 tons. Hence in justice to W. Cowan their designer, it was impossible to have bigger or more powerful locomotives at that stage. So these engines though decorative were largely ineffective. *LPC*

Below: A view at Kittybrewster of No 62, the last of the Great North's Class M of 1878, shows the locomotive in its rebuilt form after reconstruction to Pickersgill's pattern in 1904. This engine was still active on branch lines up to 1926. *W. E. Boyd Collection*

Above: In many ways the Great North's Class C engines were akin to its Class M. The driving wheels were increased to 6ft 1½in, while the gap between the driving axle and the rear axle was lessened. With the arrival of these locomotives from Neilson and Company the railway hoped to improve its main line timings, but as the engines lacked boiler power, their performance also was disappointing. They were the last outside-cylinder engines for the Great North for over 30 years, and the last to be lavishly adorned with brass work on the splashers and round the firebox. This photograph shows No 1 as built in 1878. *LPC*

Below: In due course when the Class C engines came to be rebuilt, flush top boilers, a rather shapely dome, and Ramsbottom safety valves gave them a pleasing appearance. No 1 was reconstructed in 1897 and continued to give useful service, mainly on branch line workings, until 1925. *W. E. Boyd Collection*

Above right: A breakthrough in Great North of Scotland Railway policy ensued in 1880 when Mr William Ferguson became Chairman. Notwithstanding track improvements between Aberdeen and Huntly, when a test train took 58min to cover the 41 miles, there was cause for dissatisfaction. After many arguments W. Cowan, the Locomotive Superintendent, was replaced by James Manson, the Works Manager of the Glasgow & South Western Railway who joined the Great North in 1883. A new era of locomotive design then began: Manson's first passenger engines of the Class A were built by Kitson and Company, Leeds, in 1884. Here No 66 is seen at Ballater. As the paintwork was darker than the usual livery, these engines were known as the 'black engines'. *Glen Collection*

Below right: It was obvious to Mr Manson that the Great North was sorely lacking in tank locomotives. He set about correcting this, by ordering two groups of 0-6-0T locomotives, again from Kitson and Company, in 1884-5. The first batch had only steam brakes and their main task was to shunt goods vehicles between Waterloo Goods Depot and Kittybrewster. The engines had 16in by 24in cylinders, and 4ft 6in wheels. They were robust, as well as effective locomotives and No 16 of the first batch, which were known as Class D, is seen on a shunting roster in this photograph taken c1895. *J. Peter Collection*

Above: The last three 0-6-0Ts from Kitson and Company were placed on the 'subbies' as the local trains in the Aberdeen area were popularly known. These engines all had the Westinghouse brake. As lack of water-carrying capacity was a disadvantage on the suburban workings, all three were put on to shunting when the Class R 0-4-4Ts came on the scene. This photograph shows No 38 of the group which formed Class E. Welcome features for their crews were the doors between the cab and the bunker which cut down the draughts which the 'cauld North East' generated. *LPC*

Below: This photograph of a Great North 0-6-0T of the Class E type shows No 41 in shop grey. After rebuilding in 1908, this locomotive was in service until 1934. *Glen Collection*

Above: No 15 was also one of the Great North's Kitson tanks dating from 1884. It was reconstructed in 1911 and is seen here at Kittybrewster with a leaking side tank. It was in service until 1935.
W. E. Boyd Collection

Below: Once a programme of carriage renovation and locomotive reconstruction was complete, James Manson was given permission to build two engines at Kittybrewster from parts bought from several firms. Work on the new engines was rather casual, being done when other tasks allowed. The frames were in place by 1885, but the engines first ran in 1887, and it is thought that construction largely took place out of doors. There were resemblances to the Class G (see p61) the cylinders being 17½in by 26in while the coupled wheels were 5ft 7½in. No 5 was named *Kinmundy* after the estate of the Chairman of the Great North, Mr William Ferguson. It was photographed at Aberdeen and shows the Manson boiler mountings to advantage.
A. G. Dunbar Collection

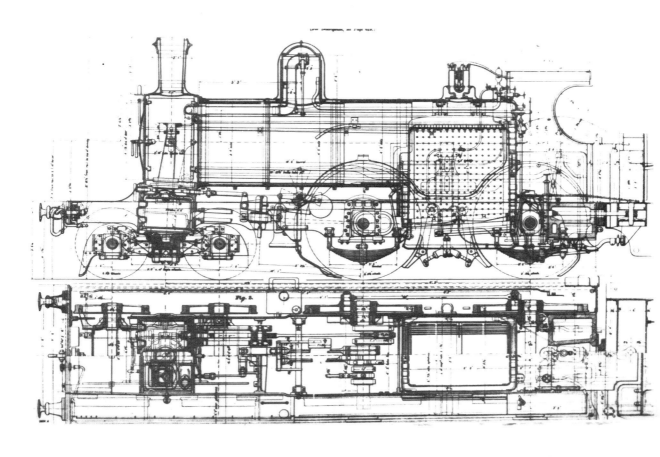

Above left: It was soon realised that engines with greater capabilities would have to be placed on the main line (which had been doubled to Insch), and on the new coast line to Elgin. The Class O was, therefore, designed to meet these requirements as well as to counter Highland opposition. Nine similar engines came from Kitson and Company in 1888. The large bogie wheels were 3ft $9\frac{1}{2}$in, the coupled wheels 6ft $0\frac{1}{2}$in and the cylinders 18in by 26in — a prototype which became almost a standard for Great North locomotives from that date onwards. This plan shows the general arrangement of these handsome engines. *Engineering*

Below left: No 10 stands beside the coal bank at Kittybrewster. This locomotive was one of the GNSR's Class O engines of 1888 that came from Kitson and Company, Leeds. In 1916 the engine was rebuilt. This class was popular with staff on account of its reliability plus ease of steaming. The bogies had swing links with double pins, quite an innovation at the time. Although meant for fast trains, soon short passenger train workings became the metier of these 'Big Kitsons'. As LNER No 6810, this locomotive was withdrawn just before World War 2. *LPC*

Above: This fine view of the elegant Manson Class P locomotive No 13 shows its bogie tender to advantage. It was a Stephenson locomotive of 1890. The coupled wheels were 6ft $0\frac{1}{2}$in, and the cylinders were 18in by 26in. The curious eight-wheeled tenders had an inside-framed bogie for the forward wheels and two rigid axles at the rear. They held 3,000gal of water and four tons of coal. They were the first tenders of their kind to appear on any British railway, and became known to enthusiasts as 'half eggs' on account of their ungainly appearance — they always seemed over large for the size of the engines! Their purpose was to give through running from Aberdeen to Elgin and back without taking water. *W. E. Boyd Collection*

Below: This other member of Class P, No 12, was photographed beside the huge coal bank at Kittybrewster. The curved footsteps were a hallmark of Manson locomotives, as were the sizeable domes, built-up chimneys, and tall Ramsbottom safety valves. From the coal stocks at Kittybrewster the Great North engines were replenished by hand crane and shovel in the years before a coaling stage was built. *LPC*

Above: The Class Q engines were also built to the plans of James Manson and came to the Great North in the autumn of 1890. The builder was Robert Stephenson and Company. This official photograph shows No 77 with its immense bogie tender. It is generally thought that these were put on the near sister Class P locomotives, while the Class Q group had six-wheelers, but this photograph of No 77 shows otherwise. As these Class Q engines had 6ft 6½in coupled wheels they soon earned the title of 'the fleers' (flyers). *British Rail*

Below: A close-up view of No 75 of Class Q of 1890 also reveals that it had one of the bogie tenders in its early days. The fall plate below the smoke box has been left open! The engine has the livery with black and white lining which was popular on the Great North in the 1890s. *Glen Collection*

Above: In 1893 the Class R 0-4-4T engines, basically to the design of James Manson with some Johnson alterations, were built for the Great North by Neilson and Company. This photograph shows No 90 of this class at Ballater, to which they ran in their early days, but stops for water were too frequent; hence their assignment became the 'subby' trains around Aberdeen. These locomotives had an extraordinary beat which resembled a short 'four in a bar'. It was recognisable a long way off and once heard could never be mistaken for any other engine. The large shed in the background was for the accommodation of the coaches of the Royal Train between journeys. *LPC*

Below: A view at Kittybrewster shows another Great North 0-4-4T engine in fine order. The locomotive is No 92, a Neilson product of 1893 which was active in the Aberdeen suburban services and other duties until its withdrawal in 1939. *A. G. Dunbar Collection*

Above: In 1890 James Johnson took over the work of GNS Locomotive Superintendent from James Manson, who went back to the Glasgow & South Western Railway. Johnson's first engines, Class S, owed much to Manson's prototypes. This Class S locomotive was photographed in its original form c1896, and it shows the high standard of maintenance which the GNS set. No 80 was a Neilson engine of 1893; it had 6ft 0½in coupled wheels and 18in by 26in cylinders. The Class S locomotives were always easy to spot on account of their two safety valves — one on the dome and one of the trumpet type on the firebox. This Johnson design

was to prove durable — No 80 was rebuilt in 1915, and was still running in 1951. *W. E. Boyd Collection*

Below: The Johnson style of boiler mountings soon vanished when the Pickersgill regime took over. Here No 82 is seen at Inverurie c1910. The liveries of the two engines present an interesting contrast. No 80 (above) is in light green with black and white lining. No 82 is in the Great North livery which was current before World War 1. Footplate edging was a rich purple brown. The white lines had gone, but the lettering of gold on red was the same. *W. E. Boyd Collection*

Above: While awaiting employment on a working, No 79 of Class S was photographed at Inverurie. One of the advantages of the small 4-4-0s which the Great North favoured was that the expense of time spent in enforced unemployment was kept to the minimum. With substantial fluctuations in seasonal traffic, at slack times many locomotives would be seen about Great North centres such as Inverurie awaiting return to duty. No 79 was one of the few GNSR locomotives to have the vacuum brake pre-1920.
A. G. Dunbar Collection

Below: William Pickersgill came to the Great North in 1894. His first engines were the Class T. A works photograph of Neilson and Company, Glasgow, shows No 112 of this class fresh from the shops. The fitment on the tender was an attachment to the communication cord which caused the alarm whistle to sound on the locomotive in an emergency. All Great North engines had two whistles. Above the hand rail was a fitting for activating a variable blastpipe. Class T was to initiate a major improvement in timing from 1896 — one engine was able to cover the 41 miles from Huntly to Aberdeen in 39min, while another took a train of 190 tons from Banchory to Aberdeen in 20min 25sec. These were certainly smart efforts. *Mitchell Library*

Above: No 95, another example of a Class T locomotive from Neilson and Company, 1895, was running to Ballater c1900. William Pickersgill was responsible for new styles of boiler mountings compared with the previous Johnson patterns, but the narrow brass band between the boiler and smokebox was retained; these engines proved most versatile and No 95 saw service up to 1947 as LNER No 6895.   *A. G. Dunbar Collection*

Below: Elgin was always a happy hunting ground for Great North enthusiasts. No 23 of the T class of 1896 was still in GNSR livery when photographed there in August 1925, and it survived the Grouping to become eventually BR No 62235, continuing to work as such up to 1950.   *W. E. Boyd Collection*

Above: The Class V engines were William Pickersgill's second design for the Great North of Scotland Railway. They were close counterparts of the Class T locomotives, but had clerestory roofs on the cabs, while the splashers were swept smoothly into the cab sheets. Five engines came from Neilsons in 1899, and the balance were built at Inverurie by the Great North. No 25 was one of the Neilson locomotives — at the outset it was No 116, but was renumbered in 1900. It was a long-serving engine being in action until 1953. *LPC*

Below: The Great North had ordered ten engines of the Class V pattern from Neilson Reid and Company, only to discover that traffic was falling. Hence the appearance of a purchaser was welcome. The five smart little locomotives were bought by the South Eastern & Chatham Railway. Here No 118 is seen carrying Great North lettering but it soon went South and the batch of locomotives became SECR Nos 676-680. *Mitchell Library*

Above: Outside Inverurie Works stands No 115, another of William Pickersgill's Class V locomotives which was a product of Neilson Reid and Company in 1899. It is in the Brunswick green livery which the Great North favoured prior to 1916. These engines were the élite of the Company in the years before World War 1 when runs at over 75mph were noted by enthusiasts, but these 4-4-0s were also as remarkable for their pleasing lines as for their consistent performance. *LPC*

Below: In 1904 the General Manager of the Great North made a recommendation that two steam railcars be placed on the St Combs Light Railway, as the branch from Fraserburgh was known. An order was given to Andrew Barclay Sons and Company, Kilmarnock, to supply the steam units, or 'motors', at £1,045 each, while the carriage sections were built at Inverurie. The engines were 0-2-2s with vertical Cochran boilers and Walschaerts valve gear. The coach portions had a central passage with slat seats on either side. In November 1905 the two units came into service — one on the St Combs route, the other on the Lossiemouth branch. Trials there, on the suburban lines round Aberdeen, and on various branches were disappointing. The following year, the coaches were converted into saloons, and as no buyers could be found for the locomotives they became stationary boilers. *A. G. Dunbar Collection*

Above: For a few months in 1915 this unusual Aveling & Porter locomotive was to be seen working the lines in Aberdeen harbour. This shunter is thought to have come from Glenlossie distillery near Elgin, but it soon returned to its original haunts when the 0-4-2 Class X tank engines came on the scene.
A. G. Dunbar Collection

Below: With the mounting pressure of war traffic in the Aberdeen docks, the Great North was short of shunters. In 1915 the railway purchased two 0-4-2T locomotives for shunting duties from Manning, Wardle and Company, Leeds. The engines had outside cylinders and were built from the maker's standard parts plus some GNS fittings. The Aberdeen harbour authorities put a weight restriction of 28 tons on the locomotives, but they were found to exceed that limit by 2 tons. The Great North however kept them as its Class Y. Subsequently another and lighter pair were bought — they became Class X. This photograph shows No 32 (formerly No 117) of Class Y. *W. E. Boyd Collection*

Above: In 1918 a new version of the 4-4-0 was introduced by T. E. Heywood who had become Locomotive Superintendent of the Great North in 1914. Six engines were ordered from the North British Locomotive Company in 1919 while two others were built at Inverurie. At first the class was known as VS but by 1920 this became Class F. All the new locomotives were superheated, with balanced slide valves on the cylinders controlled by rocking shafts, which was an old Manson practice. The group was the mainstay of the Great North's principal trains until new LNER stock came on the scene. All of Class F had names, No 54 being *Southesk. Mitchell Library*

Below: When the Class F engines came out in 1920-1 they had the black livery with red lining which was Great North practice at that time. The brass hinges on the smokebox door, together with a brass band between the smokebox and the boiler were retained. This fine photograph shows No 52, *Glen Grant,* as new in 1921. *Glen Collection*

Above right: As early as 1903, the Great North took an interest in oil fuel for locomotives, the Locomotive Superintendent being given authority to investigate its possibilities at a cost of up to £200. The experiment never got off the ground, as it soon became obvious that the cost per train-mile for oil fuel would be in excess of that for coal. During the coal strike of 1921, however, No 49 *Gordon Highlander* was adapted for the Scarab oil fuel system, and this photograph shows the engine with the oil tank atop the tender. *Glen Collection*

Below right: In 1909 a youngster with a new camera photographed No 44 of the Great North's Class K at Banff station. At the time his mother commented, 'Why are you wasting film on an old engine like that? I am sure there are far finer and bigger engines to be seen in Glasgow!' Now Banff is without a station and these locomotives are only curiosities from a Victorian past. *A. E. Glen*

Above: No 47 is seen in this picture at Elgin in the years before World War 1 when it was working on the Lossiemouth branch train. Families by the name of Paul were well-known railwaymen in the Elgin area — in fact at one time the driver, fireman and guard on this train were all Pauls. Hence the train soon earned the title the 'St Pauls Express'! Members of the Paul family are seen in this photograph. *W. E. Boyd Collection*

Below: Chasing along on a local train near Inverurie comes No 52A (formerly old No 52 but by 1920 on the Great North duplicate list). It was an old stager of Class L dating from 1876. Like so many Great North locomotives, this engine had been rebuilt in 1904, during the Pickersgill regime. Its robust appearance was matched by its capabilities after that reconstruction, as initially the class were poor performers. *W. E. Boyd Collection*

Above: A photograph taken c1890 of a 'subby' on the surburban line shows a Great North 0-6-0 tank locomotive hard at work. These engines came from Kitson and Company; in 1883 Nos 37, 38 and 41 were fitted with the Westinghouse brake for working the Aberdeen local passenger trains; the apparatus was installed on the left hand side of the bunker, but with the arrival of the Class R 0-4-4Ts these little locomotives were soon relegated to other workings. *A. G. Dunbar Collection*

Below: A new No 81 of Johnson's Class S was photographed in Huntly station c1895. The engine was built by Neilson and Company two years earlier and in this view has a trumpet safety valve, plus a second one on the dome just for good measure. The trumpet type was soon replaced by a conventional Ramsbottom safety valve, but the 'bunnet' on the dome was retained for many a year. Huntly was a rather impressive station with a covered roof forming a train shed. *L&GRP*

Above: In fine summer weather, the Class R tank engine No 89 sprints along the track out to Banchory on an excursion train of six-wheelers. This was probably an outing in connection with 'Trips Saturday' from Aberdeen. These locomotives were sprightly performers as the timings between the frequent stops on the suburban workings round Aberdeen were tight. Note the safety chains on the front buffer beam.
A. G. Ellis Collection

Below: No 114 of the V class of 1899 comes dashing along with a Great North train through the forests of the Dufftown area. All the coaches but one are in the pale cream and lake livery. The exception is the coach nearest the brake van which still has the all-lake livery which was general on the Great North up to 1896.
A. G. Dunbar Collection

Above: The versatility of the Great North's small 4-4-0s is clearly illustrated by these two photographs taken c1910. In the first, No 98 of Class T comes through city suburbs on a passenger train, which comprises an assortment of coaching stock; it contains the two saloons made from the carriage portions of the unsuccessful railcars. *Glen Collection*

Below: Then No 93 of the same class nears the same point hauling a lengthy goods train in which the line of vehicles consists almost entirely of Great North stock, whose units were small in scale but were admirably proportioned for its little engines to pull.
Glen Collection

Above: On the main line into Aberdeen a passenger train steams past. The engine is No 74 of Class O of 1888; it is sporting a Schmidt superheater fitted in 1916, and the snifting valve shows plainly on the firebox. No 74 was the first GNS locomotive to receive this type of superheating system. The first two vehicles on the train are horseboxes. After 1920, a Robinson superheater was installed on this engine. *Glen Collection*

Below: In 1925 No 65 of the old Great North's class A was seen shunting wagons at Elgin. Built in 1884, this engine was rebuilt in 1912. It was withdrawn the year after this photograph was taken. *W. E. Boyd Collection*

Above: No 107 of Johnson's Class T of 1898 was working a Great North train, probably on the line to Banchory, in the early years of this century when this photograph was taken. The train was composed of no less than ten six-wheel coaches. *A. G. Ellis Collection*

Below: No 74 of class O of 1888, with its paintwork glistening, comes spanking along on a train of eight coaches, this time on the Banchory line. The photograph dates from c1926: it shows the high standard of locomotive maintenance which the railway set in those years. *A. G. Ellis Collection*

Above: No 35, one of the Great North home products from Inverurie Works in 1914, makes light of a goods train on the main line into Aberdeen. The vehicles are of a remarkable variety. This 4-4-0 was a member of Class V which was Pickersgill's second group of Great North locomotives and the first batch on which the clerestory cab was introduced. A robust little engine, No 35 ran until 1956 as BR No 62271.
Glen Collection

Centre left: No 35 of Class V is seen again, this time near Kittybrewster on the main line to Huntly with a passenger train, of which the first two passenger vehicles are brake vans — one of an old 'low waist' type and the other a six-wheel van with apex lights in the roof.
A. G. Ellis Collection

Below left: Another Class V, this time No 34, was photographed on an Aberdeen-Macduff train, with two vintage styles of brake van behind the engine. This engine was a product of Inverurie Works in 1915. *A. G. Ellis Collection*

Above: Coming in through Kittybrewster, No 101 of Pickersgill's Class T of 1897 is seen on a goods train. The freight consists of typical products of the Great North's hinterland — whisky, timber, and all the exciting assortment of commodities that once went by rail. *A. G. Ellis Collection*

Below: In the years before World War 1 the Great North of Scotland Railway proved most enterprising in its range of excursions to encourage tourism in its area. Undoubtedly the most popular outing was to Boat of Garten. This photograph shows a Boat of Garten excursion in the Knockando area with a Class V locomotive in front. To Boat of Garten the fare was only 2s 6d (12½p) return from Aberdeen — a bargain that was irresistible to many. *A. G. Dunbar Collection*

Above: The Great North's most successful excursion train first ran non-stop to Craigellachie, 68 miles in 85 minutes, a working that was soon altered to take in a stop at Dufftown, 64 miles from Aberdeen; this was to be the longest non-stop run on the system. Originally, the objective was Kingussie, the first tour being on offer in June 1908 as 4s (20p) return! Subsequently Boat of Garten became the terminus for the outing. The excursion was available on Saturdays and Wednesdays, the Aberdeen half holiday. Such was the patronage that passengers assembled on the platform in front of locked coaches, which were opened and filled one at a time by staff. *A. G. Dunbar Collection*

Below: On a day with sea mist of 'haar' which is so prevalent on the Buchan coast, No 28 of the Great North's Class V moves slowly along on a heavy goods train, which contains over 30 vehicles. Such trains were a common sight in the years before World War 1 when almost all freight went by rail. These Class V locomotives bore the brunt of Great North traffic at that time. *Glen Collection*

Above right: A view in Aberdeen Joint station c1922 of No 103 of Class S of 1897 shows the Great North crest on the splasher — a livery detail that was encouraged after 1916 by T. E. Heywood who brought the Taff Vale black with its red lining to the Great North. *Glen Collection*

Below right: The introduction of the Class F 4-4-0s in 1920-1 was a landmark in Great North locomotive development. These superheated engines quickly won a name for their efficiency. Here No 52 *Glen Grant* in its Heywood black livery is seen on an Elgin train of 8-wheel stock in the Kittybrewster area c1922. *A. G. Ellis Collection*

Above: On the main line approaching Aberdeen Class F No 52, *Glen Grant*, of 1920, brings in a passenger train from Elgin. The two horseboxes are followed by a range of Great North coaches in which six-wheelers again predominate.   *Glen Collection*

Below: In 1908 the Great North and the Highland reached an agreement by which certain trains between Aberdeen and Inverness were worked throughout by Highland or Great North engines. The HR crews took the trains into Aberdeen but the Great North locomotives were remanned at Elgin. This photograph shows Highland Railway No 2, *Ben Alder*, entering Aberdeen Joint station on the 9.08am from Inverness, with a train consisting entirely of GNSR coaches. *LCGB (Ken Nunn Collection)*

Above: The Great North's 'Mail' train is seen passing Kintore c1908 with one of the Highland Railway's 'Big Bens', No 63, *Ben Mheadhoin,* in front. The apparatus for picking up mail bags is seen in the foreground. On 20 April 1908, when through running between Aberdeen and Inverness began, the Highland's 'Wee Bens' were frequently employed on the route, but it was not long before the Great North was warning its partner that a stronger engine would have to be put on the afternoon 'Mail' to Aberdeen as the train was not keeping good time! The Highland's answer was to place 'Big Bens' on the roster. *A. G. Dunbar Collection*

Below: A Class T locomotive, No 107 of 1898, is seen on a through train from Aberdeen to Inverness at Nairn station during World War 1. So heavy was the traffic, and so scarce were Highland locomotives, that the Great North was working trains over Highland metals — the Highland paying 1s (5p) per mile for their assistance. This engine was fitted with the combination Westinghouse/vacuum brake for the purpose of hauling the mixture of stock. Locomotives working the whisky trains from the Dufftown area were similarly equipped as the consignments went through Keith without stopping, straight to the Caledonian goods yard in Aberdeen as a precaution against pilfering! *W. E. Boyd Collection*

Above left: Ballater station was frequently the scene of Royal arrivals and departures but it was only in 1886 that a special waiting room was furnished for the comfort of Royal travellers. The station as rebuilt at that date consisted of simple timber buildings with slate roofs. In this photograph of 1895 the Duchess of York, who became Queen Mary, is seen with Prince Edward in the forecourt of the station prior to setting out in a carriage for Balmoral Castle to visit Queen Victoria. The castle was over 12 miles from the station.
By gracious permission of Her Majesty the Queen

Below left: The Royal Train is seen leaving Ballater c1905, when returning light to Aberdeen. The locomotive is a Class S of 1893. The coaches belong to the set that was built for King Edward VII and on his instructions were fitted up 'just like a yacht'. The appointments in the two Royal saloons were handsome, the King's being furnished in green and cream, the Queen's in rose and pale blue.   *A. G. Dunbar Collection*

Above: On two occasions the Great North of Scotland Railway was called upon to provide a complete Royal Train from its own coaching stock. The first occasion was in September 1903 when King Edward VII summoned a Great North train to take him from Doncaster, where he had been attending the races, to Balmoral. As this photograph shows, the train consisted of seven coaches, of which the principal vehicle was the GNSR Royal Saloon with its clerestory roof. This could be adapted for day or night use. Two eight-wheel brake vans were also employed together with coaches for the suite and staff. The same train was also assembled for the opening of Marischal College, Aberdeen.
W. E. Boyd Collection

Below: In August 1922 the Royal Train composed of the elegant West Coast stock of the early 1900s was seen making its way out of Aberdeen hauled by two Great North of Scotland locomotives, No 50, *Hatton Castle,* and No 47, *Sir David Stewart,* both of Class F of 1920-1. These are in the black livery of the Heywood era.
LCGB (Ken Nunn Collection)

Left: The Muir of Dinnet just east of Ballater was a rather bare and windswept stretch of track. Hence snow fences were erected there to protect the line. Here No 102, a Class T locomotive of 1897, crosses the Muir with the 11am train from Ballater to Aberdeen in August 1919. *Glen Collection*

Centre left: Blockages due to snow or heavy rainfall were not unknown on the Great North network. In the summer of 1915 there were serious floods in the Elgin area. As the Great North station was impassable trains were rerouted to the Highland station (which is now the only railway station in Elgin). This photograph shows an aquatic Great North Class V engine splashing through the flood water en route for Aberdeen. *W. E. Boyd Collection*

Below: As may be seen from this photograph the Moray floods of 1915 inundated the Great North of Scotland station at Elgin to such an extent that the movement of rail traffic was impossible. Here coaches stand up to the axles in water at the platform. The new circulating area had been built in 1902.
W. E. Boyd Collection

Above: The Great North's staff gather at the engine shed at Keith for this photograph which goes back to the early years of the century. The locomotive is a GNS Class T built in 1897-8. Keith was a substantial place with four roads for engines. *W. E. Boyd Collection*

Below: A smart Class V locomotive, No 25 of 1899, waits at Elgin c1911. The flags flying from the roof may have been decorations to celebrate the coronation of King George V in that year. *W. E. Boyd Collection*

Above left: This early Great North coach was a first class four-wheeler, 24ft long, having two compartments with a saloon in the centre. It came into service in the 1860s as No 34. This vehicle is in the all-purple lake livery which the Great North favoured after 1883, but initially it may have been varnished wood. *Glen Collection*

Below left: Another type of early first class coach on the Great North had three compartments and a wheelbase of only 10ft. The compartments were lit by oil lamps set in lamp holes in the roof to which the steps at the end gave access. Note the leather strap handles on the doors of this coach, which is in a light livery, probably white paint liberally coated with varnish. *Glen Collection*

Above: The six-wheeler became ubiquitous on the Great North of Scotland Railway, where it was first in use in 1882. This five-compartment third, No 71, was photographed at Ballater in 1923; it was a Johnson prototype dating from 1893. From that time the corners of window openings were smoothly curved, while a metal cowl was placed over the door ventilators. The Great North livery for coaches was elaborate — after filling or priming a brown undercoat was applied to the lower panel. On the upper and waist panels white paint was used. Then the upper panel had three coats of light cream, plus three of varnish; while three of lake plus three of varnish were put on the lower panel. The lake had a hint of crimson in it. A vermilion line separated the cream/lake colours at the waist. *A. E. Glen*

Below: The saloon sections of the railcars were parted from the locomotives and converted into saloon coaches in 1907. The reconstruction consisted of installing a new bogie, plus a lavatory compartment. The vehicles became most popular with parties of excursionists. When this photograph was taken at Ballater in 1923, Saloon No 6 was in the two-colour livery, with the frames of its characteristic rectangular top lights painted in lake. The company's monogram was applied to the lower side panel. In this view the end windows may be seen although in LNER service these were closed up and vestibule connections made. *A. E. Glen*

Above: Just after the turn of the century the bicycle craze reached its height, and with its customary enterprise the Great North prepared to cater for an influx of cyclists. In 1902 two cycle vans were constructed which comprised two racks capable of holding 14 cycles each, and were painted in the unlined rolling stock livery. The company placed these vehicles on the Ballater route in the hope that enthusiasts for the new sport would explore that area. But the craze soon passed and the cycle vans were withdrawn in 1905.

The small slate panels in the doors were for writing the cycle owners' names. *D. M. Burton Collection*

Below: A typical Great North of Scotland 10-ton wagon for loco coal, No 2719, shows its running gear, horse hook for shunting, and GNSR axleboxes. Such wagons were painted grey with white lettering and black iron work. The photograph was taken at Symington in 1919. *A. E. Glen*

Above: The Great North and the Caley formed a joint station in Aberdeen which was opened in 1867. Traffic soon outgrew its facilities so that by the 1880s complaints were being made by travellers — there were rightly objections to its congestion plus lack of protection. Then the North British began working into Aberdeen and the traffic jams on the south lines in from Ferryhill became worse. In 1899 the owning companies at last reached agreement, and an Act was obtained, but reconstruction was prolonged. The outer platforms were narrow and low, posing problems for followers of the hobble skirts fashion of the early century. This photograph shows the north end, which was rather better than the south, but even so fish trains working through the station gave it a notorious smell. The 'subbies' left from any available platform, which was most inconvenient for passengers. By 1907 new platforms were in use; in 1914 the spacious new station was complete. *L&GRP*

Below: In the north-east, Fraserburgh is familiarly known as 'The Broch', and in this picture dating from about 1900 the St Combs branch has yet to be built. The panorama extends from a vantage point up the tower of the Dalrymple Hall across the engine shed to the links and to the beach. A 4-4-0 has brought in a train from Aberdeen. On the right a steam merry-go-round has been set up on the links. *W. E. Boyd Collection*

Above: Alford station was a busy place when this photograph was taken c1910. On the left the small turntable at this little country terminus is seen, while to the right there is a line-up of the Great North of Scotland Railway's motor vehicles — including a motor charabanc and two motor lorries. By 1906 several routes for 'road motors' had been established by the Great North. The company bought the chassis and built the rest of the vehicle to suit its own purposes. The roof was used for the stowage of luggage.
A. G. Dunbar Collection

Below: Bucksburn was a stopping place on the main line from Aberdeen to Huntly, and was noted for its quarries, which are seen to the right. In Great North management, the station nameboards had white letters on a black surface. Bucksburn was also served by the 'subbies'. *A. G. Dunbar Collection*

Above: There was much activity at Bucksburn station on the day of the Sunday school outing, in which the whole village appears to be participating. The main platform had an elegant umbrella roof of steel construction with extensive glazing. *A. G. Dunbar Collection*

Centre right: Gartly was also a station on the main GNS route to Huntly and dated from the opening of that section in 1854. The style of the buildings emphasises the amazing variety of Great North stations, which in most cases appear to have been built by local contractors.
A. G. Dunbar Collection

Right: This festive gathering on the platform at Garmouth station was photographed c1910. The simple wooden buildings were typical of the Great North's little wayside stations. The offices were on the up platform (to Aberdeen) with a shelter on the down platform. By 1923, the line was single track here, the handsome timber footbridge plus the down platform being removed. The style of footbridge was typical of Great North stations.
A. G. Dunbar Collection

Above: Boat of Garten was the most south-westerly point on the Great North of Scotland Railway, where that company's metals met the Highland Railway, which owned the station at 'the Boat'. Owing to lack of agreement over the financing of a signalbox at a junction two miles north of Boat of Garten, a parallel line of track was laid for the Great North's use by the Highland Railway and the signalbox there was removed. The Great North platform was on the far right, where some of its coaches may be seen. The station has now been restored.
G. E. Langmuir Collection

Below: The Great North of Scotland Railway was an early innovator in the running of motorbuses; its first service began in May 1904 when two buses were based at Ballater to work to Braemar in connection with the trains from Aberdeen. In 1907 the Great North inaugurated a programme of tours in the summertime. The first was a 'Two Rivers Tour', but shortly other outings were on offer to excursionists; these proved very popular before World War 1. In this photograph, taken c1910, one of the GNSR Milne-Daimlers is seen in a varnish/wood livery near the Allargue Arms Hotel in Strathdon. *A. G. Dunbar Collection*

Above: One of the early Great North 'road motors' was SA 172 for which the coachwork was probably built at Inverurie by the company. The roof was used for stowing luggage, and this bus was associated with the integrated rail and road tours which were favourite excursions. The vehicle was a Milne-Daimler, with the usual GNS lake livery, and the photograph dates from c1908. *W. E. Boyd Collection*

Below: The Great North of Scotland Railway attempted to establish a seaside golfing resort at Cruden Bay, some 30 miles north of Aberdeen, in 1897. The 'Scots Baronial' style of architecture was favoured, and the hotel was open by March 1899. A tramway about a mile in length was built to connect the nearby station at Cruden Bay with the hotel. The shortness of the season plus the relative isolation of the establishment from the Scottish Lowlands were restrictions on its potential. In the Second World War the hotel was requisitioned, and in 1953 it was taken down. In this old photograph one of the two tramcars may be seen in its GNSR cream and lake livery, carrying the name 'Cruden Bay Hotel'. *A. G. Dunbar Collection*

Above: When the Grouping of the private railway companies took place in 1923, there were at first various interpretations of the new names. As can be seen from this tender, 'L&NER' with an S after the original GNSR number was the initial variant. The engine is 48a, one of the Great North's vintage Class Ks of 1866, which was subject to rebuilding in 1889, and was extant up to 1925. Just to confuse, the tender belongs to the former GNSR locomotive No 61, a **Class M** engine of 1878. *Glen Collection*

Below: Taking No 45A as the basis, plus parts from old No 48A, it was possible to reconstruct a Great North locomotive for participation in the Centenary celebrations of the Stockton and Darlington Railway in 1925. The engine was sent south with a set of seven coaches from the same period. The assemblage won much attention but it was not thought worthy of preservation. Here No 45A is seen in its GNSR livery at Inverurie in August 1925, where it became works pilot. *W. E. Boyd Collection*

Above: In the procession at the Stockton and Darlington celebrations, GNSR No 45A comes ambling along with its train of four-wheelers in the lake livery which was in vogue before 1896.
LCGB (Ken Nunn Collection)

Centre right: In much altered form the former GNSR locomotive No 40 of Class M was photographed at Inverurie when carrying a snowplough; in its LNER days the engine was No 6840. Heavy snow falls were frequent occurrences on the Great North's system, particularly affecting the lines over the Buchan plateau and the valleys of the Grampians, but snowploughs seem to have been mainly an LNER innovation.
G. E. Langmuir Collection

Right: No 6803, seen here at Elgin in August 1925, was formerly No 3 — one of the Great North's Class C engines which appeared in 1879. After a major reconstruction in 1898 the locomotive took this form, the Pickersgill boiler mountings transforming its lines. In 1927 this veteran was withdrawn.
W. E. Boyd Collection

Above: It was Great North practice to put little four-wheel tenders on the engines given tasks such as working on the Alford branch and other locations where the turntables were small. Here No 66, a Class A locomotive from Kitson in 1884, is seen in rebuilt form engaged in shunting at Kintore in 1925, the year in which it was withdrawn from service.
W. E. Boyd Collection

Below: The 0-6-0T was without much favour on the Great North system; only nine such locomotives were owned by that railway. All came from Kitson and Company of Leeds. This engine seen at Kintore as LNER No 6842 began its career as GNSR No 42 in 1889, when it was soon in service as a shunter around Aberdeen. In 1911 No 42 was reconstructed; it was then usefully employed on branch lines until withdrawn in 1936.
W. E. Boyd Collection

Above: In the summer of 1925 LNER No 6870 stands on the turntable at Macduff. This little 4-4-0 came to the Great North from Kitson and Company in 1885. It was old No 70 of Class G which was rebuilt in 1906. Although meant for hauling fast main line goods traffic this class was put to work on the Fraserburgh and Peterhead fish trains and thus won the nickname of the 'Fish Engines' a type of freight of which these locomotives smelt! *W. E. Boyd Collection*

Below: A pause at Keith for No 6805 in September 1935 gave an opportunity for the photographer to view this remarkable locomotive in LNER colours. This engine belonged to the Great North's unique Class N, and was originally No 5, *Kinmundy*, but the plate was removed in the 1900s. Built on Manson lines, this locomotive was one of only two constructed at Kittybrewster. All GNS locomotive construction was subsequently transferred to Inverurie. Here No 6805 had new styles of boiler mountings, plus Ross 'pop' valves. It was taken out of service the following year. *A. E. Glen*

Above: LNER No 6807 was at Elgin when photographed in the interwar years. It was once GNSR No 7 of the Manson Class O which came from Kitson and Company in 1888. Like many another GNS locomotive this engine was rebuilt much on its original lines in 1917 but the wing plates and Manson style of chimney were retained. This engine continued in use up to 1945. *A. E. Glen*

Below: The Great North's No 17 was also a Class O engine, and it was at Elgin as LNER No 6817 when this photograph was taken in August 1925. Five years earlier No 17 had been given a Robinson type superheater and the longer smokebox for this installation is clearly seen in this view. In LNER service the engine ran until 1946. *W. E. Boyd Collection*

Below right: A spotless engine glistens in the summer light at Elgin. No 6877 in LNER green was formerly GNSR No 77, one of the Manson Class Q of 1890. This locomotive was the first to be superheated by the GNSR in 1913 when the Schmidt type was fitted, and it soon gave proof of the superiority of the superheated over the saturated steam engine. No 77 was notable for its elegant cab with its long canopy and supporting pillars. For many years the driver of this locomotive was Alexander Davidson of Elgin, who on account of his handsome and always immaculate appearance was known as 'The Masher', and is remembered as 'a rale bull swaggerer o' a man, but aye very ceevil'. Here he stands proudly for his photograph in August 1925 beside his engine, which was always polished to perfection. *W. E. Boyd Collection*

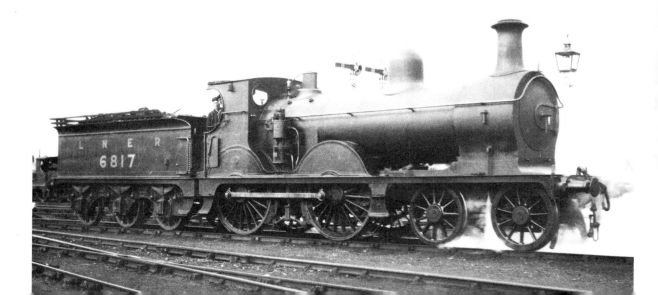

Right: With the newly erected coaling stage at Kittybrewster towering above, LNER No 6873 awaits employment with a fresh supply of coal. This engine was also a Great North Class O of 1888 from Kitson and Company, Leeds. it was rebuilt and superheated in 1920 (note the long smokebox); and was withdrawn in 1937. *Glen Collection*

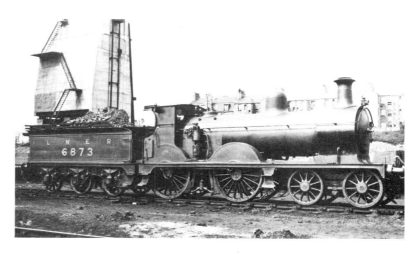

Centre right: Evening shadows fall on LNER No 6814 at Keith in 1935. This member of the Great North's Class P of 1890 was rebuilt in 1917, when a Robinson superheater was also installed. Long before the Grouping of 1923 No 14 was minus its eight-wheel tender, and here the locomotive has a Manson style of six-wheeler, plus a tender cab. No 6814 was withdrawn the following year. *A. E. Glen*

Above: In LNER colours No 6887 shunts at Inverurie. The Class R 0-4-4T engines were Neilson-built in 1893 for the suburban routes round Aberdeen. This example was formerly GNSR No 87, which was subject to rebuilding on the eve of the amalgamations in 1922. With its dome safety valve removed and with Ross 'pop' valves set on the boiler, its appearance was rather altered, but its gait was still the unmistakable gallop of the old GNSR Class R. It was taken out of service in 1947. *C. Lawson Kerr*

Below: The Class S engines on the Great North proved to be adaptable and durable locomotives. As LNER No 6880, the former GNSR 4-4-0 No 80 was working at Keith in 1928. It was a Neilson engine of 1893, which was rebuilt in 1915, when the dome cover or 'bunnet' was closed over — this gave the locomotive a new look. These Johnson engines could always be distinguished from Manson classes by their straight footsteps. No 6880 was active up to 1951 as BR No 62227. *W. E. Boyd Collection*

Above: The warmth of the day might make cab conditions stifling especially when an engine was at rest. Here former GNSR No 109 is seen at Elgin in LNER colours as No 109S in August 1925, with its cab shutter drawn. This locomotive was one of the last Class T engines to be built and was in service until 1947. *W. E. Boyd Collection*

Below: A cab view of LNER No 6900 taken from the footbridge at Craigellachie shows the simple arrangement of a typical Great North cab. As GNSR No 100 this engine was constructed by Neilson and Company of Glasgow in 1896, and was rebuilt in 1921. A Midland type of tender was used on which coal rails were subsequently set, thus raising fuel capacity. This locomotive was also withdrawn in 1947. *A. E. Glen*

Above: Riveting gear (see p13) was put on a variety of locomotives at Kittybrewster. Here in LNER management, No 6835, formerly GNSR No 35, a Class V engine which was constructed at Inverurie in 1914 in the style of William Pickersgill, shows off the apparatus while awaiting employment. Inverurie Works is seen in the background. *Glen Collection*

Below: LNER No 6825 was another example of the former Great North's Class V engines of 1899. This photograph was taken at Keith where the locomotive was waiting by the water tower. When it first came to the Great North this engine was GNSR No 116 but in 1900 became No 25. It was in use until 1953 as BR No 62260. *W. E. Boyd Collection*

Above: The Great North of Scotland's squat 0-4-2Ts which were built by Manning Wardle and Company in 1915 gave stalwart service, No 32 becoming in turn LNER No 6832 and eventually BR No 68193. It was only withdrawn in 1956. The two locomotives of the old GNSR Class Y spent their time as shunters about Inverurie, where this photograph was taken in the 1930s, and also about the Aberdeen harbour area. *Glen Collection*

Below: At the close of the First World War, the GNSR sought authority from the Railway Executive to have six new engines built. Only three were sanctioned at first but finally six were allowed. Permission was also given for two engines to be constructed at Inverurie. The eight new locomotives of Class F were superheaters and each was given a name. The first to appear was No 45, *George Davidson*, which was one of those from Inverurie and was named after the General Manager of the Great North at that time. As LNER No 6845 it is seen here at Elgin in August 1925. *W. E. Boyd Collection*

Above: In its smart green LNER livery No 6846, *Benachie*, was photographed on the turntable at Kittybrewster. As GNSR No 46, this locomotive was the last one to be built at Inverurie Works, coming from that establishment in 1921. A member of the Class F 4-4-0s, No 46 was similar to the batch of six which came from the North British Locomotive Company at that time. The engine took its name from one of the most conspicuous hills in the North East and it ran until 1955 as BR No 62274. *W. E. Boyd Collection*

Below: Shortly after the LNER takeover, this former GNSR Class M locomotive was seen working a very mixed train, probably on the Peterhead line. LNER No 6851 was of course one of the Great North's veteran 4-4-0s of 1878, having once been No 51. It was rebuilt in 1899 and was withdrawn in 1927. The stock is also 'vintage' and includes some of the company's notorious four-wheelers. *A. G. Dunbar Collection*

Above: On the St Combs branch one of the Kitson 0-6-0T engines of 1885 works a 'Bulger trainie', as the services there were known. This little locomotive, formerly GNSR No 38, was rebuilt in 1911 together with its Class E sister No 37. As a portion of the line on this branch was unfenced, the engines got cowcatchers, but their pace was so slow that it was averred they were in greater danger of being overtaken from the rear! The station is St Combs. *A. G. Dunbar Collection*

Centre right: A 'subbie' on its way into Aberdeen c1924 shows the 'L&NER' variation of that company's name as well as its former GNSR number. By this time No 88 had a Ramsbottom type safety valve, but the dome still had its characteristic 'bunnet' on the top. The coaching stock consists of six-wheelers. The photograph was taken between Kittybrewster and Hutcheon Street. *A. G. Ellis Collection*

Right: For a short time after the LNER took over, GNSR locomotives were given the letter 'S' after their number. Here No 82S, a Johnson Class S engine of 1893, works a fish train, and is seen pulling away from Portsoy in the summer of 1925. Although this locomotive had been rebuilt in 1921 it also wore the safety valve 'bunnet' on the dome at this time. As BR No 62229 old No 82 was withdrawn in 1951. *W. E. Boyd Collection*

Above: On a goods train at Boat of Garten LNER
No 6875 attracts the attention of a young enthusiast in
pre-World War 2 years. It was formerly the Great North
engine No 75 of the Q class, one of the 'fleers' which
were remarkable for their 6ft 6½in coupled wheels. In
1917 No 75 was rebuilt with a Robinson superheater,
and it ran until 1938. *Glen Collection*

Below: The versatile Class T engines were to be seen on
almost every route on the old Great North's system even
in the years of LNER management. Here No 105S,
carrying 'L&NER', was photographed at Portsoy in
1925 while hauling a goods train. As BR No 62249 this
locomotive saw service until 1950.
W. E. Boyd Collection

Above: The approaches to Cullen combined cuttings and viaducts which made the track an exciting one on which to travel. In the summer months LNER No 6899 was photographed scampering through a cutting. The locomotive was built as GNSR No 99 in 1895, belonging to that company's numerous Class T, which numbered 26 engines. No 6899 became BR No 62243, serving until 1958. *L&GRP*

Below: Coming out of Aberdeen LNER No 6901 works a passenger train for Ballater. The engine was once GNSR No 101, a Class T locomotive from Neilson and Company in 1897. The first vehicle is a very characteristic Great North type of passenger brake van and the bulk of the coaches are six-wheelers. The photograph dates from 1925. *A. G. Ellis Collection*

Above: A brief halt at Cornhill for LNER No 6826 of the former Great North's Class V of 1897 allows the guard time to confer with the driver. This engine was working on a goods roster on the line from Grange to Tillynaught, which was frequented by trains to or from the Banffshire coast, and it saw service up to 1953.
W. E. Boyd Collection

Below: LNER No 6848 *Andrew Bain* makes a neat and workmanlike impression in its green livery at Aberdeen station in August 1925. This engine of Class F, was a product of the North British Locomotive Company in 1920, appearing first as GNSR No 48. The naming of engines was rather unusual on the Great North, considering the wealth of local lore in its territory, but the Class F all got names, Andrew Bain being Deputy Chairman of the Great North of Scotland Railway just prior to the 1923 amalgamations.
W. E. Boyd Collection

Above: One of the North British built Class F locomotives of 1920-1 was No 54, *Southesk*, which is seen here passing Tillynaught signalbox in August 1925 as LNER No 6854. It was at this point that the line from Banff met the line from Elgin via the coast; the automatic tablet exchange apparatus may be seen on the left. *Southesk* took its name from the estate of a member of the GNSR board. It was withdrawn in 1947. *W. E. Boyd Collection*

Right: This interloper was one of several former Great Eastern Railway B12s which came to the former Great North network after the grouping of 1923. LNER No 8501 was photographed at Craigellachie while carrying an ACFI feedwater heater. To their firemen, who complained of the length of the cab between the coal and the firebox, these engines became known as 'hikers'. The low axle load of these locomotives however was very acceptable on the former Great North system. *A. E. Glen*

Above: The Great North of Scotland Railway took many Royal occasions in its stride. When the LNER came on the scene Great North practice was still very much on show; for example the Great North never went in for Royal Train pilots running in front of the Royal Train itself, but the company always chose two engines to haul the heavy coaching stock. On 27 August 1927, when this photograph was taken in the Joint Station in Aberdeen, the engines awaiting the Royal arrival from the south were LNER No 6852 *Glen Grant*, and No 6854 *Southesk* both in fresh paint for this special assignment. *LCGB (Ken Nunn Collection)*

Below: A Royal progress by train from Balmoral saw two sprightly former Great North of Scotland engines in the van. The locomotives in silhouette are both Great North Class F 4-4-0s and the photograph was taken in LNER years. *Glen Collection*

Top right: One of the celebrated 'trainies' on the Great North's network was 'The Messenger'. It first began to be run in 1865 as 'Queen's Messenger' when an offer was made to convey despatches and mail to Balmoral Castle from the overnight express from London while the Court was in residence, the sum of £9 2s 0d covering 80 miles of running, the courier's breakfast and a carriage and pair to the castle. This was a bargain; messages leaving London in the evening could be at Balmoral early the following morning. Previously Royal 'Messages' were brought by pony trap over the hills from Perth. To inaugurate the rail service, a locomotive was painted in a tartan livery. In 1883 the 'Queen's Messenger' was the subject of an acrimonious court case as the landowner at Crathes objected to the fact that it failed to stop there although the Act of Parliament for the railway stated that *all* trains must do so!

Passengers could join 'The Messenger' by taking first class tickets, and in so doing might rub shoulders with august personages journeying to Balmoral. The train, as the 'King's Messenger', is seen here at Cults in 1927 with LNER No 6854, *Southesk*, in front. The service was stopped in 1937 when a motorcar took over these royal duties.
LCGB (Ken Nunn Collection)

Above right: On a Sunday afternoon a fine line-up of former Great North engines in LNER livery was photographed at Kittybrewster. The Great North of Scotland Railway was rather averse to running trains on the Sabbath and activity was minimal in the interwar years. The first in line is LNER No 6822, then

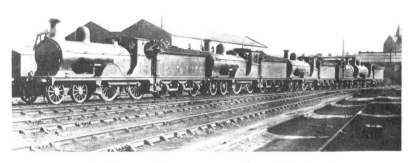

No 6846 *Benachie,* followed by two 4-4-0 former GNSR Class Ts, with an 0-6-0 Class E tank between them.
Glen Collection

Below: Once the LNER regime became established a green livery was chosen for its passenger locomotives. The former Great North employees were only too happy to paint their engines green again,

regardless of whether they were on passenger workings or otherwise. Thus the 0-4-2T LNER No 6844 (once No 44 of Class X) was seen at Kittybrewster sporting a green livery. Of course when this came to the notice of officialdom there was a fuss. The other locomotive is LNER No 6845, *George Davidson*, one of Class F of 1921, which in this view is in black paint. *Glen Collection*

Above: In the shelter of the engine shed at Macduff on the Banffshire coast LNER No 6898 rests in summer weather. This typical locomotive of the Great North era was a Class T of 1895, and was originally No 98. It was subject to reconstruction in 1920 and ran until 1948 as BR No 62242. *A. G. Dunbar Collection*

Below: In prewar years Keith shed was often a focus of attention for railway enthusiasts. Here a former Great Eastern Railway 4-6-0 seems a giant among the little Great North 4-4-0s in their LNER livery. As may be seen, former Class T locomotives predominate as LNER D41s. *Glen Collection*

Above: This carriage was formerly a Great North six-wheel semi-corridor composite coach with two first class and three third class compartments. The two lavatories to serve these classes were in the centre of the vehicle. This was a Pickersgill pattern of c1898 which was initially a first class semi-corridor on GNSR major trains. *A. E. Glen*

Below: This six-compartment composite corridor coach was from the early Pickersgill phase which began in 1898, when bogie stock came on to the Great North's network for the first time. The new carriages were 48ft overall, with Fox's pressed steel patent bogies. This example was seen in its LNER colours in 1935 on a train at Boat of Garten. *A. E. Glen*

Above: So popular were the two small saloons (only 40ft 7in in length) which were converted from the railcars, that two larger saloons were constructed in 1907. These were 48ft long and third class throughout, and saw service on the twice-weekly outings to Boat of Garten. The saloon layout was a favourite with parties, enabling the Great North to offer buffet meals on that excursion. This was the only 'restaurant' facility on a Great North of Scotland train until 1922. Here one of these carriages, LNER No 7661, is seen at Boat of Garten in the interwar years.   *A. E. Glen*

Below: Top lights were first incorporated on Great North coaching stock in the railcars, and the saloons of 1907. These features then became standard on new carriages for the railway. This six-compartment semi-corridor coach had two toilets; the opaque glass was etched with the GNSR monogram. The characteristic S-bend coach handles show clearly in this photograph which was taken at Boat of Garten in 1935.   *A. E. Glen*

Above: The semi-corridor non-vestibuled coach was a popular style on the Great North's network. This eight-compartment third class carriage, 52ft long, had one lavatory. It also had the high roof line with top lights which was typical of the more modern designs of Pickersgill coaching stock on the Great North. The vehicle was photographed at Boat of Garten in LNER livery as No 7420. *A. E. Glen*

Below: After 1907 the cove roof was given more curvature as the new electric lighting for carriages made housings for oil lamps superfluous. It thus became feasible to raise the height of the roof line. This Heywood style of six-wheel coach of 1914 was a five-compartment third, 33ft 6in overall on a 20ft wheelbase. Although in the LNER's simulated teak finish it still revealed its Great North origins. *A. E. Glen*

Above: To accompany its trains of six-wheelers, the Great North had matching six-wheel passenger brake vans which were neat little coaches. This vehicle bearing LNER No 742 was on view at Elgin and was Westinghouse-fitted for branch line working. When in GNSR service this brake van was in the two-colour livery, while the lamp housing above the lookout was painted red. Gold leaf transfers with red and brown were used for numbering and for lettering on all GNSR coaches.
A. E. Glen

Centre left: Just as the Great North locomotives were light in character, so were the vehicles they hauled. This little eight-ton flat truck was photographed at Aberlour when carrying LNER No 800460. The brakes were worked from one side of the wagon by means of the long lever which is seen in this view. The horse hook tow rope bracket was placed on the solebar, and shows just above the axlebox to the left. *A. E. Glen*

Left: A group of 10-ton goods vans with steel solebars was constructed by the Great North before World War 1. The basic frame was 18ft 0in long on a 10ft 6in wheelbase. This van was photographed far from Great North territory — at Bowling on the River Clyde — and although it was in LNER employment its ancestry was plain, as these vehicles had a robust appearance due to their external framing.
A. E. Glen

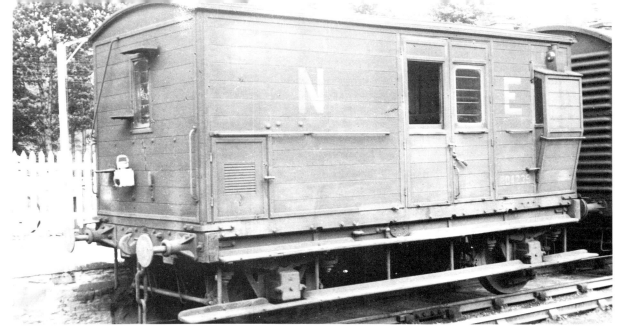

Above: The Great North's goods brake vans were noteworthy as they were completely enclosed. There were guard's lookouts or 'duckets' which projected at one end of the vehicle. The small door with the ventilator louvre was a dog box, as these brake vans also served as accommodation for a drover plus a dog when livestock was in transit. Sometimes brake vans were also used as goods vans for the carriage of small consignments of goods between stations. In GNSR years the livery was dark red with black running gear and ironwork. As an LNER vehicle, No 804239 was at Craigellachie in the 1930s. *A. E. Glen*

Below: The Great North of Scotland Railway's tramway, which was a link between Cruden Bay station and the hotel of that name, was taken over by the LNER. The two tramcars were painted in the varnished teak livery of that company. When the line to Cruden Bay was closed to passenger traffic in 1932 the little tramcars were used to convey hotel goods and laundry as Cruden Bay was the central laundry for the LNER in Scotland, but after the outbreak of World War 2 they were withdrawn. *A. G. Dunbar Collection*

Above: The station buildings at Banchory were stone built and substantial. When the railway there was first open for traffic in 1853 this station was a terminus. As this photograph shows, it was notable for its high booking hall and spacious forecourt as much as for its pleasant setting. *J. Peter Collection*

Centre left: The little station of Cambus O' May on the line to Ballater was in harmony with the sylvan beauty of that route. It was a simple timber structure with a slate roof, and once again emphasises the astonishing variety of Great North of Scotland station architecture. *J. A. N. Emslie*

Below left: Woodside, just out from Aberdeen, was one of the 14 small original stations on the Great North's first line, which went to Huntly. This station was subsequently reconstructed for the use of suburban trains after the 'subbies' began running in 1887. It was closed to traffic in 1937. *A. G. Dunbar Collection*

Right: Pitmedden also lay on the mainline to Huntly, some 10 miles out from Aberdeen, and took its name from a nearby estate. The brick-built signalbox controlled the level crossing, and two small verandahs were placed on the platforms to shelter passengers.
J. L. Stevenson

Right: Grange was one stop from Keith on the main line to Elgin. As was customary at Great North stations, the principal offices were on the up platform — the reason being that most passengers would join trains into Aberdeen; thus on the down platform there was only a small shelter. In this photograph from LNER years, there had been little alteration at Grange — even the 'Notice as to Trespass' still carries the title 'Great North of Scotland Railway Company'.
J. Peter Collection

Right: Fyvie was a Great North station between Rothie Norman and Auchterless on the line to Banff. Although following general Great North principles with two 'pavilions' and a central booking office, this station unlike so many others was brick-built.
J. L. Stevenson

Left: Towiemore was typical of the distillery halts in the famous 'golden triangle' of Banffshire. It is on the line from Keith to Craigellachie which now goes no further than Dufftown, for goods traffic only. Towiemore took its name from the neighbouring distillery which was built in the promotional boom of the 1890s; when the 'whisky bubble' burst in 1899 the Great North's traffic to and from the area slumped and was only recovering shortly before World War 1. *J. L. Stevenson*

Centre left: Craigellachie was the junction for the line 'via the Glen' to Elgin, and the route to Nethybridge and Boat of Garten. The station was built for the opening of part of the latter railway in 1863. This view shows the approach viaduct to the station. *J. L. Stevenson*

Below: Craigellachie station kept its typical GNSR timber footbridge for many years. This photograph shows the up line (left) and the branch to Boat of Garten (right); it also reveals how sinuous the track was at this point. *Glen Collection*

Above: The stations on the line to Boat of Garten were as well known for their remarkable names as for their country charm. Knockando was always a tongue twister for those from the South; its Gaelic meaning is *the market hill*. These stations were closely associated with the numerous local distilleries, and one of the two such establishments at this village may be seen.
J. L. Stevenson

Right: Travellers familiar with the rural lines of Morayshire will remember this station: 'Bla-acksboat' was the porter's call. The place name came from the ferryboat which formerly plied on the river at this point. In this photograph from the 1950s the Great North 'Notice as to Trespass' was still intact — *plus ça change*!
J. L. Stevenson

Left: Advie station on the line to Boat of Garten was rather impressive for such a rural locality. The reason was it proximity to Tulchan Lodge a shooting box which was well known to members of the Royal family, particularly to King George V when he was Prince of Wales. For such excursions to Tulchan the Great North of Scotland Railway marshalled its own Royal Train.
J. L. Stevenson

Below left: Nethybridge was in the most western corner of the GNSR rail system. It was built in 1863, and was first known as Abernethy. The station was a simple one with a small goods shed, signalbox, and level crossing gates.   *A. G. Ellis Collection*

Above right: Lossiemouth lay on a GNSR branch $5\frac{1}{2}$ miles from Elgin which was opened for traffic on 10 August 1852 as the Morayshire Railway. This shows the station arrangement with the goods yard (centre) and the station offices (right). A single line was also built to serve the fishing harbour; this is seen in the foreground.   *J. L. Stevenson*

Right: Urquhart was also on the coast line to Elgin and lay between Garmouth and Calcots. It was a trim country station with a little goods yard mainly serving the farming economy of its hinterland.
J. L. Stevenson

This picture: Findochty was a little seaside station on a stretch of the line along the coast from Cullen to Elgin which was open as far as Garmouth in 1886. Its timber offices and small goods yard were most characteristic of lesser Great North stations.
J. L. Stevenson

Above: Banff station was a terminus by the harbour which came into use when the railway to that town was open by 1859. The station was enclosed against the onslaught of wind and weather on the Banffshire coast. In 1950 BR No 62251 was working on the route; being the former GNSR engine No 107 of Class T of 1898 it gave a unique 'Great North' flavour to the place, which had altered little over the years. *G. E. Langmuir*

Left: The cavernous interior of Banff station with its timber roof was an unmistakable feature of the town. This photograph shows the up platform as it was in 1964. *G. E. Langmuir*

Above right: Ellon Junction was situated where the line to Cruden Bay and Boddam took off from the Formartine and Buchan route some 15 miles to the north of Aberdeen. The branch was open to traffic in 1897, but was not a profitable one; by the 1940s it was open for goods traffic only.
G. E. Langmuir Collection

Centre right: At Mormond, which is seen in this photograph in its British Railways days, the station offices and house were combined so that staff were in quarters 'above the shop'! Here BR No 62228 (formerly GNSR No 31, an Inverurie-built Class V of 1910) approaches Mormond with a local train working on the Fraserburgh line in 1950.
G. H. Robin

Below: St Combs was a little coastal terminus on the branch line from Fraserburgh which was opened to traffic in July 1903. Like many later Great North stations the premises were simple timber ones. The purpose of the line was to serve a 'suburb' of Fraserburgh. This view of St Combs station was taken in July 1951. *A. G. Ellis*

Left: Many Highland rivers are fast-flowing and tortuous, with steeply sloping valleys. A wrought iron structure had to be built at Carron, where the railway and road were to cross the river. The strong masonry abutments support the seven wrought iron sections of the arch.
J. L. Stevenson

Centre: This substantial bridge was a replacement for an early arched viaduct across the river Deveron near Rothiemay, on the GNSR line from Huntly to Keith. As may be seen it has masonry abutments carrying lattice work girders. The arches of the original viaduct are visible beyond the new structure in this photograph. *J. L. Stevenson*

Below: The approach to Cullen was awkward, the line having to skirt the harbour and cross a steeply sloping valley. High embankments and viaducts were essential as this photograph shows. Now that the track has all been removed these features remain a remarkable example of the art of civil engineering of which the railway was capable.
Messrs Balfour, Cullen

Right: Fraserburgh was a coastal terminus on the Great North and its sizeable timber signalbox was a reflection of the importance of the station on the Formartine and Buchan section of the railway. The line was open for traffic from 1862, and was shut as a result of implementation of the Beeching Report after 1963. *J. L. Stevenson*

Below: The interior of Fraserburgh signalbox shows the frame with its levers and the track layout for the station and yard. The cabin was one of the larger installations on the Great North system. *J. L. Stevenson*

Above: The signalbox at Portsoy was an unusual example of the Great North's early pattern having a masonry base with a timber superstructure. There was also a branch line to Portsoy harbour — its track is seen in the background in this photograph. *J. Peter Collection*

Left: Mintlaw was on the branch line to Peterhead and its tall timber signalbox was typical of many on the Great North's system. The apparatus for automatic tablet exchange is seen to the right. Most Great North boxes grew flourishing tomato plants in the summer season! *Glen Collection*

Right: BR No 62256 brings the whisky train into Boat of Garten c1949. This train came from the Dufftown area; it took consignments of malt whisky south. Regrettably it was prone to pilfering, casks being broached en route, particularly in those years when Scotch whisky exports were given priority, and home supplies were very scarce. No 62256 was once a Great North Class T of 1898, carrying No 112 for that company. It was rebuilt in 1916 and was out of service by 1952. *A. E. Glen*

Top: The convergence of the GNSR and Highland single lines just south of Broomhill, Inverness-shire, was the scene of much rivalry. Here A. E. Glen stands at the location of the former signalbox with a typical GNSR post to his right. The photograph was taken in 1961. *G. E. Langmuir*

Above: In perfect summer weather BR No 62251 was seen preparing for the road near the engine shed at Elgin in 1950. This locomotive was formerly one of the Great North's Class Ts, No 107 of 1898, and was another veteran performer on the lines of the North East. *Glen Collection*

Above: The crew were busy taking coal and water on to the tender of BR No 62271 on an August day in 1949 when this photograph was taken at Boat of Garten. This locomotive was once GNSR No 35 of Class V; it was constructed at Inverurie in 1914, and was active up to 1956. *A. E. Glen*

Below: Making a brave show of smoke, BR No 62267 pulls away from Elgin on a local 'trainie' for Lossiemouth in 1954. As was common Great North practice this engine has a tender cab; it was originally No 29 of Class V of 1909, and was an Inverurie-built locomotive which ran until 1956.
G. E. Langmuir Collection

Above: BR No 62264 works a long goods train on the line from Keith in September 1954. This engine began its years with the Great North in 1898 as No 115, continuing with the LNER as No 6915. It was one of the versatile, hard-working Class V locomotives which saw almost 60 years of service. *J. Peter Collection*

Centre right: In the 1950s BR No 62270 was photographed on the St Combs branch while working on a passenger train from Fraserburgh. Two of the coaches were former GNSR vehicles. The locomotive was built at Inverurie Works as one of the Class V engines; a batch of eight was constructed as part of a renewal programme on the Great North in 1914. On completion this engine was No 35; it was still in steam in 1956. *J. Peter Collection*

Below right: For many a year the thickset little 0-4-2T locomotives of the Great North were a familiar sight about Aberdeen harbour or at Kittybrewster. This engine began to work on the GNSR as Class X locomotive No 44, coming from Manning Wardle and Company in 1915, and it was still active early in 1959 as BR No 68191. Its sister, No 68192, became the last GNSR engine in regular service, working until 1960. *W. E. Boyd Collection*

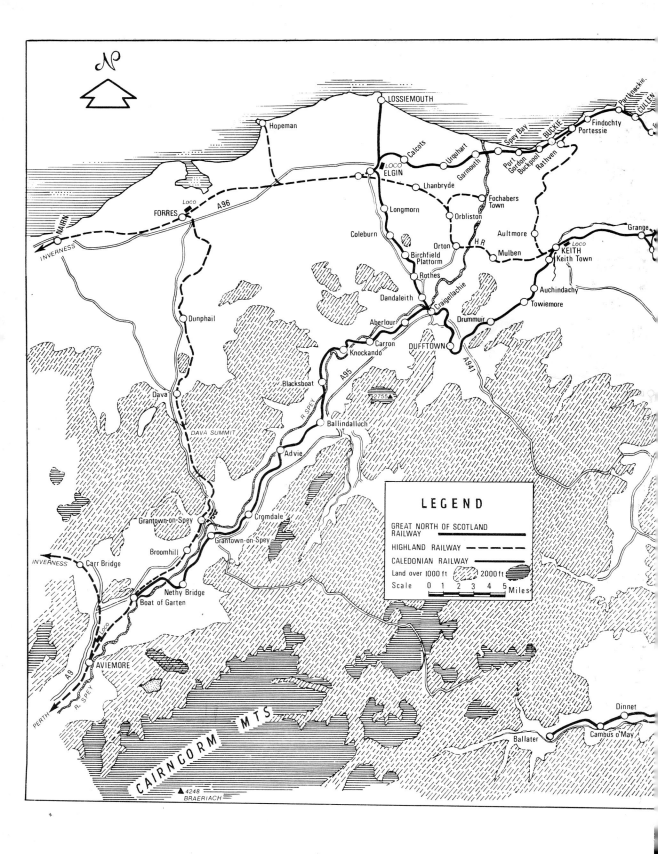